Clearing the Colours

A Play

James Vollmar

A Samuel French Acting Edition

SAMUELFRENCH-LONDON.CO.UK
SAMUELFRENCH.COM

Copyright © 2006 by James Vollmar
All Rights Reserved

CLEARING THE COLOURS is fully protected under the copyright laws of the British Commonwealth, including Canada, the United States of America, and all other countries of the Copyright Union. All rights, including professional and amateur stage productions, recitation, lecturing, public reading, motion picture, radio broadcasting, television and the rights of translation into foreign languages are strictly reserved.

ISBN 978-0-573-02378-1

www.samuelfrench-london.co.uk

www.samuelfrench.com

FOR AMATEUR PRODUCTION ENQUIRIES

UNITED KINGDOM AND WORLD EXCLUDING NORTH AMERICA

plays@SamuelFrench-London.co.uk

020 7255 4302/01

Each title is subject to availability from Samuel French, depending upon country of performance.

CAUTION: Professional and amateur producers are hereby warned that *CLEARING THE COLOURS* is subject to a licensing fee. Publication of this play does not imply availability for performance. Both amateurs and professionals considering a production are strongly advised to apply to the appropriate agent before starting rehearsals, advertising, or booking a theatre. A licensing fee must be paid whether the title is presented for charity or gain and whether or not admission is charged.

The professional rights in this play are controlled by The Sharland Organisation Ltd, Manor House, Manor St, Raunds, Wellingborough, Northamptonshire, NN9 6JW.

No one shall make any changes in this title for the purpose of production. No part of this book may be reproduced, stored in a retrieval system, or transmitted in any form, by any means, now known or yet to be invented, including mechanical, electronic, photocopying, recording, videotaping, or otherwise, without the prior written permission of the publisher. No one shall upload this title, or part of this title, to any social media websites.

The right of James Vollmar to be identified as author of this work has been asserted by him in accordance with Section 77 of the Copyright, Designs and Patents Act 1988

CLEARING THE COLOURS

First produced at the Stephen Joseph Theatre, Scarborough, on 24th June 2005 with the following cast of characters:

George	John Branwell
Dora	Eileen Battye
Danny	Neil Grainger

Directed by Kate Saxon
Designed by Pip Leckenby

CHARACTERS

Dora
George
Danny

The action takes place in a seaside resort guest house and a snooker club

Scene 1   Dora's sitting-room
Scene 2   The snooker club. The next day
Scene 3   Dora's sitting-room. The next day
Scene 4   The snooker club. The following week

Time—the present

PRODUCTION NOTE

The play was originally set in a North-East seaside resort but it can be set in any seaside resort. Any topical references in the text can be changed to accommodate this.

CLEARING THE COLOURS

Scene 1

The sitting-room of Dora's guest house in a seaside resort

It is the house of a seaside landlady. There is a window upstage. The furniture comprises a sofa, a small table. On a nearby shelf or sideboard, or perhaps hung on the wall, are two framed photographs: one of an elderly man, the other of a cat

George and Dora enter. Both are around sixty. George carries a tray of tea things: pot, cups, etc. George looks around

George You've done something to this room.
Dora Redecorated, that's all. Young lad down the road did it for me, just started in the business.
George Nice ...
Dora Dennis always hated decorating, bless him. (*She glances at the photo*)

Pause. George puts the tea tray down on the table. Dora serves

Dora It's good to see you again, George. Never know when you're going to be around these days.
George You know me, here and there.
Dora Never could get used to dry land could you? (*Peering outside*) I've just put some washing out but I'm sure it's going to rain. What do you think?

George We're by the North Sea, Dora. Anything could happen.
Dora That's a lot of use. I thought you were supposed to be an old sea dog! At the very least I expected the odd pearl of nautical wisdom.
George You're the one with the pearls of wisdom. (*Beat*) Who's that god who's supposed to be in charge of the sea? Neptune, isn't it?
Dora I think so.
George (*playfully*) Not on first name terms with him are you?
Dora Cheeky devil. There's only one God, George. He's supposed to be in charge of the whole universe.
George Yeah I forgot divine intervention had been nationalized. Well anyway, if Neptune wants a good laugh around these parts he doesn't go looking for a comedian, he listens to the weather forecast. (*Beat*) Thought you'd be able to tell anyway.
Dora Whatever it does it won't bother me. That's more important than knowing everything.
George I suppose so.
Dora That tea OK for you, George?
George Just right. Thanks. (*Beat*) Busy at the moment?
Dora Ticking over. I've got a couple of actors in, and a bird watcher. Out of season, can't complain. The bird watcher gets up early, the actors get up late. It all works out. (*After a beat she chuckles*) One of the actors is in a rock 'n' roll show at the Palace. I can hear him singing Elvis Presley songs in the shower. You know Elvis would have been older than us if he'd been alive now. Quite a thought — him collecting his pension at the post office in Memphis or wherever ... (*Beat*) Is there something on your mind, George?
George Can't I just drop by and visit an old friend?

Pause. She frowns playfully. George knows he can't fool her

I wanted to talk to you about someone. A lad I've got on my books. Danny Miller. Snooker player. Very good. Going in for the qualifiers in Blackpool next week, for the British Open. If he gets through it'll be TV, world ranking, everything. The big time.

Scene 1

Dora Sounds exciting. Well done, George.
George Oh ... you get lucky sometimes ...
Dora You deserve it, all the work you've done helping people.
George I'm a personal manager, Dora, not Mother Theresa. I'm supposed to be in business. I just seem like a charity because I've never really had anyone successful before. Soon as anyone starts to make it big they move on and leave me with the no-hopers — boxers who get knocked out one time too many and turn to the bottle, comedians who stop being funny and turn to the bottle. Believe it or not I even had a ventriloquist once who fell out with his dummy. Attacked the damn thing! Knocked its head off, literally. Then he felt so guilty about it he turned to the bottle. Thinking about it I should have cut out any pretence of being in the entertainment business and become a bloody publican straightaway. Least I'd have made some money out of my clients.
Dora George. Without you none of these people would have got anywhere. You're the one who goes out to all those sleazy clubs and sweaty gyms to watch them. Those big agents just hang around in their posh offices like vultures while you do all the hard work.
George Yeah well. I'm glad to do what I do. At least I can sleep at night.
Dora But this lad's different, obviously. The snooker player.
George Oh yes, he's different. He's really got it, Dora. I've never seen talent like this, not in anyone. The real thing. You can tell when you see it.
Dora Where did you find him?
George His dad was on my books actually. Boxer. Good amateur in his day. Had a couple of pro fights but never really made it. You can guess the rest.
Dora Does it involve a bottle?
George It did, until the pubs stopped serving him. Then it was a six pack on a park bench. In the end he left Danny and his mum to fend for themselves ... (*Beat*) Danny was just a kid, but I could see he had something. Raw energy. He'd put on a pair of boxing gloves, kick a football, swing a cricket bat, anything ... But it wasn't till

I saw him with a snooker cue I knew what it was inside him fighting to get out. I showed him the basics — I was a decent player in my day, had some coaching from Fred Davis. Danny was twelve years old when he beat me for the first time, and I've never got close to him since.

Dora What about his mum? How does she fit into all this?

George She never took much interest in Danny to be honest. Not after his dad ... (*Pause*) Took to spending a lot of time in the pubs and clubs, steady stream of men friends ... you know the sort of thing ...

Dora Were you one of them?

George (*a little shocked*) No.

Dora Come on, don't give me that "butter wouldn't melt" look. We're both grown-ups.

George It's not that ——

Dora What you got up to on your shore leave in Bangkok is your business, George.

George What's Bangkok got to do with it? This is the East Coast. (*Pause*) His mother and I ... there was nothing between us, all right?

Dora So why are you telling me all this?

George I want to help this lad, Dora. I don't want to see him make the same mistakes his father made. I've seen it so many times.

Dora I don't know much about snooker.

George I'm not looking for a coach. That's not the sort of help Danny needs.

Dora I can never remember which ball goes where. I remember watching it once and thinking, "No wonder this game takes so long, every time someone pots a ball that fellow with the white gloves keeps putting it back on the table." (*Indicating the photo on the sideboard*) Dennis used to like a bit of snooker. (*Intrigued*) I could see if I can pick anything up ...

George Now, you're losing me ...

Dora Never mind — the concept of sport probably doesn't exist in the spiritual dimension anyway.

George The point is, I think you can help him. Like you helped me.

Scene 1

Dora You helped yourself, George.

George You gave me the key.

Dora That's often all it needs.

George I want him to see that. I want him to see that winning's no use if you can't enjoy it. You've got to believe you're worth it. If you don't believe that, if the winning's all there is, you'll just destroy yourself. Dora, I don't want this lad to end up another George Best or Alex Higgins or Mike Tyson. (*Pause*) That's why I'd like to send him to see you.

Dora Does he want to come and see me?

George (*a little sheepishly*) Actually I haven't mentioned it to him yet.

Dora George ...

George Let me talk to him, all right?

Dora George, young lads today aren't going to be interested in what I've got to say. All they care about is plugging themselves into a computer and raving away to this hip hop do wap ... bebop ... do wah diddy diddy or whatever they call it.

George (*amused*) I think you've just covered fifty years of popular music in one sentence. (*Beat*) I really think a lot of this lad, Dora. I really think he can make something of himself.

Dora (*with a sigh of resignation*) Well, don't expect miracles. Sometimes you win. Sometimes you lose.

George I know. Thanks, Dora. I'll have a word with him.

Dora (*peering outside*) I do believe it's started to rain. Who'd run a B and B, eh? Never know if you'll survive one year to the next.

George You'll be here till global warming washes you away, you know you will.

Dora Bookings are down for this summer. They all want Majorca or Ibiza these days, don't they? *Guaranteed sunshine* to go with the *guaranteed happiness* all those adverts on the telly are promising them. All of a sudden seasons don't seem to matter any more ... (*Beat*) Are you ready for some more tea now, George?

The Lights fade to Black-out. Music

SCENE 2

The snooker club. The next day

A rather run-down snooker club. There is a chair or bench seat in one corner. On the wall there are a rack of cues, a blackboard with lists of players and matches, and a sporting calendar

Danny and George enter. Danny is around eighteen years old, confident, restless. He is carrying a snooker cue and a tabloid paper, open at the sports page

George Great session, Dan.
Danny Yeah. Thanks.
George It's all looking good.
Danny Yeah ... no problem. (*Reading*) Looks like Newcastle are after that Italian striker ...(*Reading again*) Can't pronounce his name ...
George Like I say, work on your safety, that's the only weak area.

Danny bridles a little at this, looks up

I mean ... relatively speaking.
Danny Yeah, OK.
George I mean it, Danny. Think more between shots. That moment's quiet can make all the difference. Remember Arthur Ashe, at Wimbledon? Closing the eyes? (*He does, briefly*) Course you don't. What am I talking about ...?
Danny George, snooker's about potting balls. You pot the balls there's no need for safety.
George Your potting's brilliant
Danny Well then ——
George An all round game, Dan, that's what wins championships. You know I'm talking sense.
Danny Yeah. I know. You're talking sense. I'm gonna win this match, George. I know it ——
George Danny, nobody knows anything for sure.

Scene 2

Danny I can't lose. I'm up against some bloke on his third attempt to qualify. He works as a carpet fitter for God's sake.
George We've all got to earn a living, Dan.
Danny I know. I used to sell mobile phones, didn't I? I'm just saying, that's all. You've got to want it. (*He thinks*) Didn't Arthur Ashe die anyway?
George Everybody dies.
Danny (*tongue in cheek*) Thanks, George. I can see now why the Samaritans never took you on.
George OK, well, that's enough for today.
Danny George. I've been thinking. I'd really like to get a dog. You know, to race.
George A greyhound?
Danny No, a poodle. There's big money in poodle racing at Sunderland dog track. Of course a greyhound!
George First things first. Let's win the qualifier before we start buying dog biscuits all right ?
Danny Yeah, all right. I'm just saying.
George We'll think about it, OK? Anyway. I'm going to get some lunch. What are you doing now?
Danny Just chilling out.
George Fancy a bite?
Danny No you're all right. There's some racing on the telly this afternoon. I'll probably meet a couple of my mates later for something to eat and a few drinks.
George Yeah, well don't overdo it.
Danny All right I won't overdo it.
George Sorry. I don't mean to sound like your mum. I mean ——
Danny (*more amused than angry*) Yeah, if my mum could care less about where I was you would sound like her.
George I'm sorry, lad ...
Danny That's OK. We both know the score.

An uneasy pause

George Did you ring her up? About coming up to Blackpool with us?

Danny Yeah ... (*Sarcastically*) Unfortunately she'll be in Majorca with one of her boyfriends. But she wishes me luck.
George Well that's something.

Danny gives a contemptuous snort

It's been hard for her too, Dan. Left on her own.
Danny Well I'd say she's making the best of it, wouldn't you?

An uneasy pause

George This is the last lap, Dan. We need to stay focused.
Danny Yeah yeah. I am. Totally focused.
George Why don't you go to the cinema or the theatre later? Relax.
Danny On my own?
George Good way of switching off. I could come with you if you like.
Danny I've never been to the theatre in my life.
George What about those pantomimes I took you to when you were a kid?
Danny It's not Christmas, George. Anyway I'm a bit old for singing along and shouting, "He's behind you!"
George It's good fun. Chance to be a kid again ——
Danny I don't want to be a kid again. Anyway, when you get older you realize the only reason ... he's behind you is 'cos he wants to shaft you while you're not looking.
George You're a born romantic, you know that? All I'm saying is ... try and relax a bit, just until the match. Drinking's not relaxing. Not really. You think it is but it's not.
Danny OK. I'll check what's on at the Odeon if it'll make you happy. I'm not gonna let you down on this, George.
George I know.

Danny goes to leave

Oh Danny — before you go. You've always trusted me, haven't you? With your management and coaching like?

Scene 2

Danny 'Course.
George When I put you on to that snooker pro in Bradford.
Danny Sure. He taught me a lot.
George There's someone else I'd like you to see before the qualifier.
Danny Another coach?
George In a way. (*Beat*) It's a lady.
Danny Snooker coach!
George No. Something else.

Pause

Danny (*laughing*) You're joking!
George (*realizing what is implied*) Oh no ——
Danny I wondered what all this stuff was about relaxation. Old navy habits die hard, eh?
George I didn't mean that ...
Danny Those long, steamy nights in Bangkok ——
George Why's everybody going on about Bangkok all of a sudden? I spent most of my time in Tilbury ——
Danny I don't need to pay for it, George. When I get through to the UK finals I'll be able to have any girl I want.
George I thought you'd already got a girlfriend?
Danny Yeah. Stacey. She's all right.
George Just all right?
Danny You know how it is, George. Things are changing. You do the best you can.
George Meaning — poor old Stacey's history as soon as you get your face on the telly?
Danny Meaning — who can say? (*Beat*) Listen to you. How long, did your marriage last, remind me? Away at sea, playing snooker — same thing. (*Beat; with some remorse*) Sorry ...
George No ... Who am I to preach? Anyway, you know that's not what I meant. About the lady.
Danny So if it's not — Justine with the French lessons, who is it?
George A friend of mine — Dora. She runs a guest house, on the sea front.

Danny Why would I need to see her? Does she do a good full English breakfast or something?
George She does actually — but she's also a kind of psychologist you might say ...
Danny Psychologist! I'm not bonkers, George ——
George It's not like that. This is the twenty-first century for God's sake, Dan, lots of sportsmen use psychologists! To enhance their performance, improve their concentration. Anyway psychologist's probably the wrong word.
Danny What's the right word?
George (*tentatively*) Dora's a sort of — spiritual healer.
Danny A what?
George Hold on a minute ——
Danny I don't believe this!
George Danny ——
Danny You're sending me to a bloody fortune teller?
George It's not like that ——
Danny I'm a snooker player, George. I win matches by potting balls, not by reading the tea leaves.
George Danny, that's not what it's all about. It's about — using your potential ...
Danny George ——
George Look, listen for a minute will you? Just listen.

Danny shrugs

George When I came out the navy I had a bad back. It was killing me. All I had to look forward to was a life on disability benefit and pain killers. The NHS didn't want to know. I tried it all ... acupuncture, chiropractors the lot. And yes, I really did have a massage in Bangkok, though not the sort everybody seems to think. Anyway, back home somebody recommended I go and see Dora. I thought it was a load of rubbish at first but I reckoned I had nothing to lose. I mean she didn't even charge anything. So I went. (*Beat*) When she touched me it was like a warmth going through me. She said I had a ... blockage in my ... healing channels ... said I was holding a lot of things in, a lot of pain. I started thinking

Scene 2

about things from the past. It was like it all came bubbling up, like she stirred up the mud on the bottom of a pond or something. I just broke down in tears, sobbed my eyes out. I tell you, Danny, I walked out of that house without pain and I've never had any since.

Pause

Danny George. I haven't got any pain ——
George Not in your body maybe.
Danny The past is the past. It's gone ——
George We think it is ——
Danny It's gone ——
George We like to pretend ——
Danny I don't pretend, George. My dad was a drunken bastard and my mum's a slag. Is that honest enough for you? (*Beat*) Look. I'm gonna win this match next week by my own efforts and I'm gonna go on and be world snooker champion by my own efforts and I won't care about them, like they never cared about me. It'll be me who's done it, me alone. (*Beat. More subdued*) And you of course. I won't forget that.
George Then listen to me now. When a runner's on the blocks, it's those few seconds before the gun goes off that gives him the edge. The running's only part of it. It's the stillness. The balance. Like pulling back an arrow in a bow. The pulling back's as important as the letting go.
Danny (*amused*) George, I think you've been watching too many Kung Fu movies. (*In an Oriental voice*) It's the stillness, Grasshopper. (*More seriously*) Look, I know you mean well but I don't need this.
George That's the thing, Danny. You don't know you need it, until you get it, then you wonder how you ever lived without it.

Pause

Danny What was your pain then? You said you were holding in a lot of pain.

George (*a little uneasily*) It's not about me. It's about you. What have you got to lose? You don't have to believe in anything.
Danny I don't.
George That's OK ——
Danny When you're dead you're dead.
George Ay, well, you might be right. But it's not about that. It's about life ... now. (*Beat*) Oh I don't know much about God and stuff: I just know there's more to us all than we think. Like we're living in one room of a house and keeping all the others locked up ... (*Thoughts triggered, he holds back*) Helping your game, Dan, that's all I'm thinking about. Pretty soon now you'll need to start digging deeper. It'll be a top professional across the other side of the table, not someone straight out of the local Working Men's Club. You'll need an edge. We ought to be thinking about the next step.

Pause. Danny seems a little uneasy

Danny Yeah, actually ... I wanted to talk to you about that. I was going to leave it till later but seeing how we're talking about things now. (*Pause*) I've been approached. An agent. In London. Nothing definite.

Pause

George (*subdued*) Right. Well I didn't expect this. Not quite so soon anyway.
Danny There's nothing definite, George. You know I'll see you all right. I mean without you ...
George Yeah ...
Danny Like you said, we're in a different league now. We need people who are used to moving in those kind of circles. There's sponsorship and all that to think of. This bloke reckons ... well, like I said, there's nothing definite. (*Beat*) Tell you what. I'll go and see this old bird, if it makes you happy.
George Whatever ...
Danny (*brighter*) I'll go. All right? I'll go. I want to.

Scene 3

George It's up to you, Danny. Do what you think best, all right? (*He makes to leave*) I'm going to get some lunch.

George goes

Danny is left alone, a little guilty. The Lights fade to Black-out. Music

Scene 3

Dora's sitting-room. The next day

Dora enters with Danny. He is edgy, restless

Dora Sure you won't have some tea, love?
Danny No thanks. I'm all right.
Dora You can sit down.

Pause. He does not sit

Danny Look. I'll level with you. I'm only here because George wanted me to come.
Dora That's all right. I'm surprised you came at all to be honest.
Danny So, if it's all the same to you. I'd like to get this over with as quick as possible, all right? Read your tea leaves or whatever you do and then I can get back to what I do.
Dora (*chuckling*) There's no tea leaves, love. You don't need to refuse a cup of tea for that reason.
Danny It's OK. I'm not really thirsty.
Dora All right. It would help if you sat down though.

They sit

Dora So, tell me a bit about yourself.
Danny I thought you were the one who was supposed to know everything.

Dora Nobody knows everything, love.
Danny (*peering outside*) Why's your washing out? It's raining.
Dora It won't last forever.
Danny Not exactly a good advert though is it?
Dora I think you've got the wrong idea about this. Didn't George tell you ...?
Danny Yeah, he told me. You're a spiritualist.
Dora A spiritual healer. Sounds a bit fancy for my liking really. Let's just say I've got a ... gift. Not something I expected, or even asked for. Like you, I suppose, with your snooker. (*Beat*) It's very exciting I must say. The British Championships.
Danny Yeah. You know anything about snooker?
Dora Nothing at all.
Danny Great.
Dora My grandson watches it all the time on the telly. I must get your autograph for him before you go.
Danny I'll send you a photo. We're getting some done.
Dora (*regarding Danny*) Thank you, very kind.
Danny What are you looking at me like that for?

Silence. Just a smile from Dora

George told you all about me anyway, didn't he?
Dora He told me a few things ...
Danny So life is crap. You hardly need a crystal ball to tell me that. It's what you make of it that matters.
Dora So what's the point of it all?
Danny The point is to use your skills, what's up here — (*he taps his head*) — to earn enough respect so that you can shut it all out.
Dora What if it finds its way back in again?
Danny It won't. (*Beat, he looks around*) Well. I must say this is all pretty tame. I thought at the very least you'd get in touch with my dad or something. I was looking forward to that. I'm not scared of him. I can tell him just what I think of him.
Dora Where do you think he is now?
Danny Dead. Six feet under.
Dora So why did you ask me to get in touch with him?

Scene 3

Danny I was taking the pi— mickey, all right? You wouldn't get any sense out of him anyway. Even if he was in heaven he'd have found a way to smuggle some booze past the angels by now.
Dora He's in a better place I can assure you.
Danny Better than Whitley Bay! Well, he has done all right for himself.
Dora Anyway I'm not going to get in touch with him, I don't do that kind of thing.
Danny Good. 'Cos as far as I'm concerned he can rot in hell. Or Heaven. Or Whitley Bay for that matter.
Dora You didn't love him?
Danny Now how did you figure that out?

Pause

Dora What about your mum?
Danny What about her? (*Pause*) When my dad walked out on us she went to pieces. Just what I needed at ten years old as you can imagine.
Dora What about since then?
Danny Well — she's consistent I'll give her that; a real tower of strength ...

Pause

Dora I don't know exactly what else George wanted me to talk to you about.
Danny Well that makes two of us.
Dora It's only because he cares about you. He thinks a lot of you, you know. He doesn't want to see your talent go to waste.
Danny It won't go to waste.

Pause. She looks at him, unsettles him a little

Dora Danny, have you ever been playing snooker or driving a car or something and it feels like you're not really there? That it's not really you doing the playing or the driving. That it's you being driven. Everything goes right, like it's all been mapped out for you.

Danny You mean like ... being in the zone? Yeah I've felt that.
Dora What do you think is driving you then? What's keeping you safe?
Danny Me.
Dora But you're not doing, anything, are you? Not consciously.
Danny It's still me. Who else can it be?
Dora What if you could get to that place more often? Or if your whole life was lived with just ... one foot in that place.
Danny I never thought about it. It just happens.
Dora All the problems we have, all the stress and the hatred and bitterness we feel, they stop us reaching that place ——
Danny I don't believe that. I like a bit of stress. I feed off it. (*Looking at the photograph*) Who's that?
Dora My husband. Dennis. He died six years ago. Cancer. Next to him is Jerry, our cat. He died last year. (*Suddenly curious*) Have you got any pets, love?
Danny No. Look — I should go. Thanks for your time but I'm all right as I am.
Dora Don't run away.
Danny I'm not running.
Dora Say what you think.
Danny I'm not thinking anything.

Pause

Dora You're thinking: how could she call herself a healer when her own husband died under her very nose?
Danny Look ——
Dora That's what you're thinking.
Danny All right, it's what I'm thinking, OK? But you said it, not me.
Dora (*with a steeliness as yet unseen*) You think I'm some kind of sugar plum fairy, some phoney seaside fortune teller? When Dennis died I told God in no uncertain terms what I thought of him. Two thousand years of buggerin' about and you can't do any better than this, you senile old fool ... letting a good man die in pain!

Scene 3   17

Danny (*surprised and pleased*) Good for you! You tell him.
Dora I did, don't worry. (*After a beat, amused*) George told me a story once. You know George, always got his head in some book or other. He told me there were once some Jews in Poland or somewhere like that who were very religious, performed all the right ceremonies as God had told them to. And yet their village still suffered a terrible famine. So they put God on trial for negligence. In a proper court. Found him guilty, of letting his people down. And the next day six cartloads of grain arrived.

Pause

Danny What's that supposed to mean?
Dora Nothing really. It's just a story I like. Humility's a bit dull, isn't it? Either God's God or he isn't. Praying shouldn't be like writing a letter to the Council. When you deal with the top man you want some action. You need to show him what you're really made of. (*Beat*) After a while I realized Dennis hadn't really gone anywhere. It was just like he'd popped down the shop or to the football or somewhere ... He's not here, but he's still around, if you see what I mean. (*Beat*) The channels aren't clear, that's the problem. There's all kinds of ... stuff in the way. We should have been told how to get rid of it, but I'm afraid there's a lot of people who'd much rather keep us in fear, sitting in churches begging God to help us. Half those people only go to show off their Sunday best anyway. Give them a dose of real ... spirit they'd run a mile. (*Beat*) Look at George. He's been all over the world. But he's been all over the world with his mind open. He wants to learn. That's what matters. God doesn't want you to be a pushover, Danny, he just wants you to play fair. (*Beat*) Clear the colours. Isn't that what you say?
Danny Yeah, it's what we say. What's that got to do with it?
Dora Once you get to that special place, winning or losing won't be what it's all about. You'll be in the game, forever. You'll never lose, not deep down.
Danny Yeah, well, losing's not on my agenda. Don't worry about that.

Dora Maybe not now. But you're going to lose, one day. Everybody does. The trick is to be disappointed, not defeated. Your real value's not just a score someone else hangs round your neck.

Pause

Danny Look ... I've gotta go. (*He starts to leave, stops, looks at her*) You're all right you know. I thought you'd just be some wacky old bird with a pack of cards and a teapot. But you don't stand any nonsense, do you?
Dora We've stood it long enough. (*Beat*) Come here a minute, love.

Danny goes to her. She puts her hands on his head, closes her eyes

Yes, there's a lot of pain there.

A moment's silence. Danny starts to become uneasy, agitated. He breaks away

Danny All right all right. That's enough, I promised George I'd come along and I have. I've gotta go.
Dora All right, love. Come back another time if you want to.
Danny Thanks but ... here. (*He takes out a ten pound note*)
Dora I don't want your money, love.
Danny Give it to the stray cats or whatever.
Dora (*amused*) You must be psychic. My friend Jean's having a fund-raiser for the local sanctuary next week. (*She takes the money*) She can tell them the smoked salmon's on you. (*Beat*) Did you say you had some pets, love?
Danny No.
Dora Not ever?
Danny What's that got to do with anything? Look, I've gotta go.
Dora Well good luck. In your match.
Danny Thanks. (*He starts to leave, turns back*) Aren't you going to tell me if I'm going to win or not?
Dora (*chuckling*) Someone else has decided that already, love.

Anyway, what do I know? I'm just a wacky old bird who can't even choose the right day to hang her washing out. (*Peering outside*) Will you look at that rain?

The Lights fade to Black-out. Music

Scene 4

The snooker club. The following week

George enters, excited. He is speaking on a mobile phone

George Hallo, Dora. ... Yes. I wanted to let you know that Danny's through. He's qualified. He was fantastic. Top form. ... Yes, we've just got back. I'm at the club. ... Yes, it'll be TV and everything ... Just thought you'd like to know. Thanks for all your help. ... OK. I'll let you get on. ... OK. I will. ... Yes, he'll be here if you want to pop in. You know where we are? The snooker club. ... OK then. See you later. 'Bye.

Danny enters. He seems a little weary, hungover, from his success

George Dora. I just told her the good news. She said to tell you "well done".
Danny Thanks.
George She might call round if she's got time. You had a word with the lads?
Danny Yeah. I said I'd see them later, buy them a few drinks.
George You could let yourself off practice today, Dan. Relax. Enjoy the moment.
Danny Yeah well, later maybe. (*Beat*) I've got a few things to do.
George You made an impression, you know. She thinks a lot of you. Dora.
Danny Great.
George I'm glad you made the effort ——

Danny I'm not going back, George if that's what you're getting at.
George OK. It's not a problem. She just wanted to let you know she's happy for you that's all.
Danny Right, well, that's great. Thanks. (*He thinks*) She was all right actually. Got a bit of something about her. You wouldn't mess with her, would you?
George No, you wouldn't ... (*He smiles*) Now we need to start thinking ahead. We've got a couple of months. Tomorrow, we need to start work. I've had a word ——
Danny George — it's all fixed up.
George What ...?
Danny That bloke I was telling you about. The agent. From London ...?
George Ah ...
Danny It's ... well I've decided to sign with him.
George Right. Well. I hope you've thought this through.
Danny I've thought it through. We've gone through it all — line by line.
George Line by line ...?
Danny The contract.
George Who's "we"?
Danny Me and him.
George You and him. So you're just going to sign yourself away.
Danny George ——
George It's OK. I'm just trying to look out for you that's all. Like I always did.
Danny I know. It won't be the end. I mean I'd still like to keep you on, in an advisory role.
George Well thanks, but in my experience those kind of things don't usually work. Like having two managers of a football team.
Danny There'll be some compensation for you. I insisted on that.
George Whatever ...
Danny I'm sorry, George. It's just ——
George That's all right. It's all right. Really. I was looking to retire from this business in a year or two anyway. All I've got on my books now is you, two boxers and a magician. He'll probably

Scene 4   21

    disappear before long anyway. (*He chuckles*) Get it? Magician? (*Wearily*) It's the way I tell 'em ...
Danny I really appreciate what you've done for me. I mean I couldn't have ——
George (*interrupting*) Yeah — yeah ... (*Pause*) You've got a great future, Danny. I wish you all the best, you know that.
Danny Yeah. I know.

They embrace, a little self-consciously

George You were good yesterday.
Danny Thanks.
George I mean really good. In the zone.
Danny The zone? Never heard you use that word before.
George It was special.
Danny I've been in the zone before.
George Yeah but not like this.

Pause. Danny is suspicious

Danny Hold on. I know what you're getting at.
George She helped you, Danny. I can see the difference.
Danny There's no difference. Just practice. And being focused.
George Whatever you say. (*Beat*) Didn't you feel something though? When she touched you?
Danny (*uneasily*) Maybe ... You can make yourself believe anything if you want to. And like I told ... Madame Dora — there's nothing she can see in her crystal ball that she couldn't see looking out of any window, any day of the week. So there's a lot of pain! The secret is knowing how to use it. I use it, George. The anger. It's what gives me the edge. I don't want anybody to take that away from me. Sitting around smiling ear to ear ... at peace with the world, that doesn't win trophies. Look at Ronnie O'Sullivan. Roy Keane. Lance Armstrong. They've got the edge.
George What about Alex Higgins, Mike Tyson, Paul Gascoigne...?
Danny They're not me George.

George I'm just saying — the edge is fine as long as you don't fall over it.
Danny I'm not falling over anything.

Pause

George No. I believe you. I really do think you'll make it. 'Cos you're not stupid, Danny. With some people the door's closed and you know it always will be. With you the door's open. Just a little bit maybe. But more than you think. (*Beat*) I was like you once you know. Dad hard as nails. Mum who didn't try hard enough. But I'm glad I left that door open, I'll tell you — to learn things. (*Pause*) I think she helped you, Danny. Let's leave it at that, all right?
Danny No George, we won't leave it at that. I won that match because I'm good. That's the only reason. OK? (*Pause, he thinks*) Sparky old bird I'll give her that. Like I said, I quite liked her in the end. But when you think about it, she told me nothing she couldn't have already got from you.
George I wouldn't trick you, Danny.
Danny No ...
George Well then. (*Pause*) Surely you know me better than that
Danny Yeah I know, but Malcolm said ... I mean this agent I'm talking to ... I told him about it — going to a healer like. He said it wasn't a good idea. Said it wouldn't do my image any good.
George Your image?
Danny Yeah. Malcolm said we gotta be thinking about an image now. (*Preening a little*) He said my image was the cool guy from the streets, the wrong side of the tracks, you know?

George scoffs

It's the way things are, George. This game's not just old men in waistcoats any more.
George There's a difference between image and the real thing, Dan. Cliff Thorburn really did hustle for money in the Vancouver pool halls. I think he rode freight trains as well. That's the real thing ...

Scene 4

Danny Yeah well, all I've got's the Gosforth Labour Club and the ten-thirty to Newcastle Central, so we've all gotta do the best we can, yeah? Anyway Malc says if the press got hold of it — that I'd been to a faith healer — they'd crucify me ... I mean look what they did to Glenn Hoddle.

George You think they won't get you some other way when they decide they're fed up with you? Danny, the people who write those kind of stories are no better than parasites ... Oh it'll be all wine and roses at the start — a Page Three Girl on each arm, a Ferrari and a Tudor-style house in Essex. Then they'll start sniffing around for the dirt.

Danny They can sniff all they like.

George It's the mob culture, Dan. "He earns more in a week than I do in a year so I have the right to knock him down." You hear it every Saturday afternoon on every Premier League football ground in the country.

Danny It goes with the territory, George. And the territory's what matters. That's something they haven't got, and never will have.

Pause

George (*wistfully*) Danny from the mean streets! Remember when I took you to see Father Christmas in his grotto, and the illuminations at Blackpool ...?

Danny (*a sigh of resignation*) All right, how much do you want?

George (*shocked*) What ...?

Danny How much do you want? Not to sell your story. Not to make me look like some Oliver Twist orphan wimp ——

George (*angrily*) Don't insult me, Danny. I wouldn't give those scum the satisfaction.

Uneasy pause

You really think I'd do that? After all we've been through.

Danny No — look I'm sorry, George. I don't feel good about this.

George Just live with it, Danny. That's what I've got to do.

Danny Malcolm said he'd have a word with you soon.

George Yeah well, he knows where to find me.
Danny He says he knows somewhere I can get a dog as well. A greyhound. He's got them for some of his footballers. (*Beat*) Anyway. I've got a meeting ...

Dora enters, with coat and shopping bag, a little breathless

Dora I was going round the shops anyway, thought I'd pop in, see if I could catch you. I just wanted to say many congratulations. Well done, love. George told me.

She and Danny kiss. He is a little uncomfortable

Danny Yeah. Thanks. Thanks a lot. (*Uneasily*) Look. I need to do some things. Nice to see you again.
Dora I never did get that autograph, for my grandson.
Danny I'll send you a photo, yeah? What's his name?
Dora Simon.
Danny No problem. I'll let George have it.
Dora Thanks. (*Beat*) So ... I expect you two have got a lot of plans to make.

Uneasy pause

George Danny's moving on, Dora. To new management.
Dora Oh, that's a shame.
George Things change. Nothing stays the same forever.
Dora That's very true. Well I wish you all the best, love.
Danny Thanks. Anyway ...
Dora You never answered my question by the way. (*Beat*) Excuse my nosiness. It's just been playing on my mind for some reason. Won't leave me alone ...
Danny I haven't really got time to tell you my life story now. (*Beat, intrigued nevertheless*) Sorry — which question?
Dora About whether you had any pets.
Danny (*irritated*) As it happens I am thinking of getting a greyhound, to race. (*He wants to leave*) Now if you don't mind ——

Scene 4

Dora I meant before. When you were a child perhaps. Sorry. I know it's painful ——
Danny (*a flash of anger*) It's not painful. It's just annoying when someone keeps asking you the same stupid questions.
Dora Sorry, love. It's just something I'm picking up. A little black and white dog following you around ...

Pause

Danny (*looking around*) What are you talking about?
Dora (*amused*) Not here, love. In the spiritual dimension. He's with you all the time. Jack Russell perhaps. I'm not very good with dogs.

Danny is shocked. Pause

White, with a black patch over his left eye?
Danny This is a trick right? (*He looks at George, in anger and disbelief*) You couldn't just let it go could you?
George What ——?
Danny Skipper. She's talking about Skipper. You know she is. I had him when I was a kid.
George (*the memory coming back*) That's right. I remember Skipper ——
Danny Don't give me that amnesia act! (*Simmering*) Look at you. Both of you. You're pathetic ——
George Steady on, Dan ——
Danny Don't insult my intelligence, George. You told her about my dog just so she could bring him out like — a rabbit from a bloody hat. Thought you could hang on to me that way did you? Get me where it hurts?
George Dan. I hardly remember him ——
Danny You're a sad old man, George.
Dora Steady on, love ——
Danny Don't "love" me, you old witch. You told me nothing you couldn't have already got from him, (*Pause, painful thoughts*)

That dog was my best friend. The only one who never let me down. When he died I buried him myself. Dug the hole, laid him in it. Well my dad was nowhere around, was he? Big tough guy, crying into his beer in some backstreet bar. Droning on about the good old days when he ... could've been a contender.

Pause

Dora I'm sorry, love, I didn't mean ...
George Danny it's not what you think ——
Danny Don't talk to me, George. Ever again. You want to speak to me you contact me through my new management right? I'll pay you off, I owe you that, but that's it. From now on, you and me are finished.

Danny leaves

George and Dora are shocked and silent for a moment or two

Dora I'm sorry, George. Me and my big mouth. (*Pause*) I'd better go. Come round sometime, when things have settled down, we'll have a chat ...
George Just help me out with this, Dora. I never told you about his dog did I?

Pause

Dora No, you didn't tell me. Like I said, he's just ... around ... Expect he'll watch out for Danny, as best he can. Like you did, George. But you can only do so much for someone. (*Looking outside*) Bit brighter now. Two bookings today as well. Two families, for a week in August. Looking for a traditional English seaside holiday. That's the thing with this business, you can never tell ...

The Lights fade to ——

——Black-out

FURNITURE AND PROPERTY LIST

Scene 1

On stage: Sofa
Small table
Framed photo of an elderly man, framed photo of a cat

Off stage: Tray of tea things (**George**)

Scene 2

On stage: Chair or bench seat
Rack of cues and sporting calendar on wall
Blackboard with list of players and matches on wall
Snooker cue, tabloid paper open at sports page (for **Danny**)

Scene 3

On stage: Sofa
Small table
Framed photo of an elderly man, framed photo of a cat

Personal: **Danny**: ten pound note

Scene 4

On stage: Chair or bench seat
Rack of cues and sporting calendar on wall
Blackboard with list of players and matches on wall
Mobile phone (for **George**)

Off stage: Shopping bag (**Dora**)

LIGHTING PLOT

Property fittings required: nil
2 interiors

To open: Full general lighting on sitting-room

Cue 1	**Dora**: "... for some more tea now, George?" *Fade to black-out*	(Page 5)
Cue 2	To open Scene 2 *Bring up lighting on snooker club*	(Page 6)
Cue 3	**Danny** is left alone *Fade to black-out*	(Page 13)
Cue 4	To open Scene 3 *Bring up lighting on sitting-room*	(Page 13)
Cue 5	**Dora**: "Will you look at that rain?" *Fade to black-out*	(Page 19)
Cue 6	To open Scene 4 *Bring up lighting on snooker club*	(Page 19)
Cue 7	**Dora**: "... you can never tell ..." *Fade to black-out*	(Page 26)

EFFECTS PLOT

Cue 1 **Dora**: "... for some more tea now, George?" (Page 5)
  Music for scene change

Cue 2 **Danny** is left alone (Page 13)
  Music for scene change

Cue 3 **Dora**: "Will you look at that rain?" (Page 19)
  Music for scene change

A licence issued by Samuel French Ltd to perform this play does not include permission to use the Incidental music specified in this copy. Where the place of performance is already licensed by the PERFORMING RIGHT SOCIETY a return of the music used must be made to them. If the place of performance is not so licensed then application should be made to the Performing Right Society, 29 Berners Street, London W1.

A separate and additional licence from PHONOGRAPHIC PERFORMANCES LTD, 1 Upper James Street, London W1R 3HG is needed whenever commercial recordings are used.

www.ingramcontent.com/pod-product-compliance
Lightning Source LLC
Chambersburg PA
CBHW070454050426
42450CB00012B/3276